ACADIA NATIONAL PARK

A T R U E   BOOK

by
Wende Fazio

Children's Press®
A Division of Grolier Publishing
New York   London   Hong Kong   Sydney
Danbury, Connecticut

A ringed bill gull
perches in Acadia
National Park.

Reading Consultant
Linda Cornwell
*Learning Resource Consultant
Indiana Department
of Education*

Content Consultant
Deb Wade
*Chief of Interpretation
Acadia National Park*

Author's Dedication
For Weeters, my best friend

Visit Children's Press® on the Internet at:
http://publishing.grolier.com

Library of Congress Cataloging-in-Publication Data

Fazio, Wende.
    Acadia National Park / by Wende Fazio.
        p.   cm. — (A True book)
    Includes bibliographical references and index.
    Summary: Describes the history, landscape, wildlife, and activities
available for visitors to Acadia National Park.
    ISBN 0-516-20659-1 (lib. bdg.)   0-516-26425-7 (pbk.)
    1. Acadia Nationa Park (Me.)—Juvenile literature. [1. Acadia National
Park (Me.) 2. National parks and reserves.] I. Title.
II. Series.
F27.M9F28   1998
974.1'45—dc21   97-24129
                                                                      CIP
                                                                       AC

Contents

Acadia National Park 5

An Island Is Born 8

The People of Mount Desert Island 12

Plant and Animal Life 18

Your Visit to Acadia 30

To Find Out More 44

Important Words 46

Index 47

Meet the Author 48

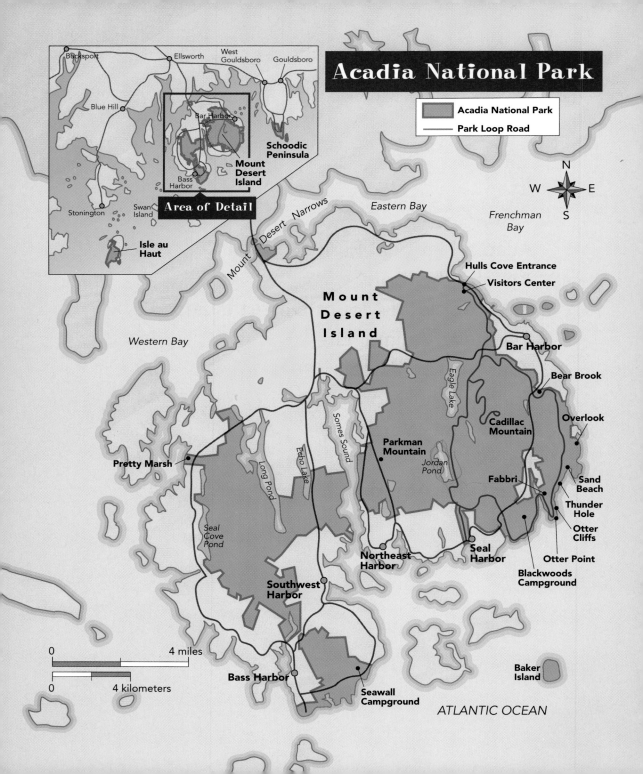

Acadia National Park

Acadia National Park
Park Loop Road

Bucksport
Ellsworth
West Gouldsboro
Gouldsboro
Blue Hill
Bar Harbor
Schoodic Peninsula
Mount Desert Island
Bass Harbor
Stonington
Swan Island
Area of Detail
Isle au Haut

Mount Desert Narrows
Eastern Bay
Frenchman Bay

Hulls Cove Entrance
Visitors Center

M o u n t D e s e r t I s l a n d

Western Bay

Eagle Lake

Bar Harbor

Bear Brook

Cadillac Mountain

Overlook

Pretty Marsh

Somes Sound

Echo Lake

Long Pond

Parkman Mountain

Jordan Pond

Fabbri

Sand Beach

Thunder Hole

Otter Cliffs

Seal Cove Pond

Northeast Harbor

Seal Harbor

Otter Point

Blackwoods Campground

Southwest Harbor

0   4 miles

0   4 kilometers

Bass Harbor

Seawall Campground

Baker Island

ATLANTIC OCEAN

Acadia National Park

Acadia National Park is made up of three parts. Most of the park is located on Mount Desert Island, off the coast of Maine. A small portion is on the mainland of Maine. This area is called Schoodic Peninsula. A section of a small island to the southwest of

Mount Desert Island is also part of Acadia National Park. This island is called Isle au Haut and can only be visited by taking a ferry boat.

Acadia National Park occupies more than 40,000 acres (16,000 hectares). Mount Desert Island is surrounded by the Atlantic Ocean and several other smaller bodies of water. Along Acadia's rocky coastline, you will find colorful granite cliffs and cobblestone beaches. You will also find

A peaceful sunrise outlines this aerial view of the islands near Acadia.

mountains rising up from the ocean and deep lakes cut into valleys. There are meadows and marshes, and dense evergreen forests.

An Island Is Born

Millions of years ago, huge pieces of rock on the ocean floor were flattened by heat and pressure from inside the earth. This action created a hard, pink rock called granite, which can be seen today all over Acadia's coastline. The heat and pressure also caused a dark, heavy volcanic rock to form. This rock is called basalt.

Pink granite and loose rocks cover the coastline of Acadia National Park.

Over the ages, glaciers carved away at Acadia. Glaciers are huge masses of ice that move slowly across land and mountains. Jordan Pond, Long Pond, Echo Lake, and Eagle Lake were created by glaciers.

Somes Sound is just one area in Acadia created by glaciers.

Somes Sound is a fjord that was also created by glaciers. A fjord is a long, narrow passage of the ocean between high cliffs.

Today, the ocean continues to shape Acadia. Day and night it pounds the rocks at Otter Cliffs.

The water constantly grinds up the rocks. Eventually, the pieces become so fine that they mix with tiny pieces of shell. The ocean carries this fine mixture of rocks and shells to Sand Beach, Acadia's only accessible sandy beach.

Sunset at Sand Beach

The People of Mount Desert Island

The Wabanaki people were living on Mount Desert Island long before the European explorers discovered it. The Wabanakis hunted, fished, and gathered plants and berries.

Jesuit priests were the first Europeans to settle on Mount

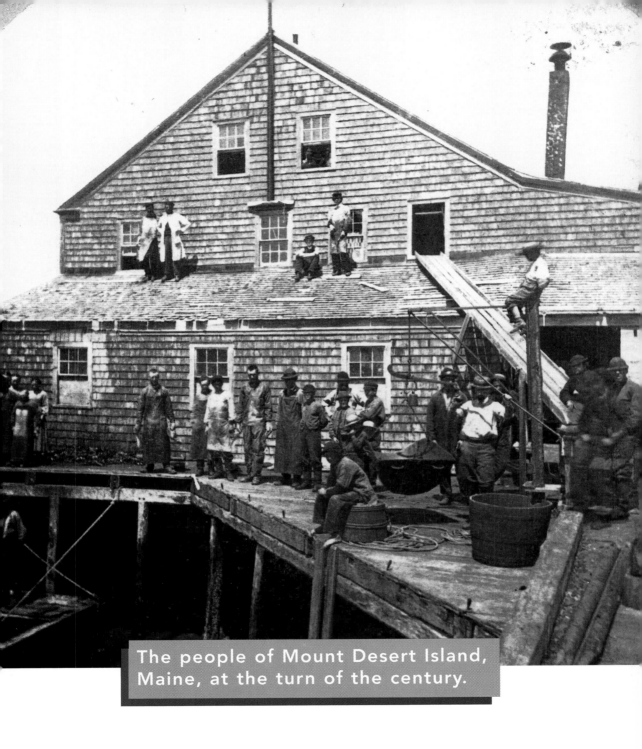

The people of Mount Desert Island, Maine, at the turn of the century.

Jesuit priests attempted to teach Christianity to many Native Americans in the region.

Desert Island. They were warmly welcomed by the Wabanakis. The Jesuits wanted to build a mission on the island and teach Christianity to the

Wabanakis. But soon after the Europeans arrived, most of the Wabanaki people became sick and died from smallpox and other European diseases.

European settlers continued to arrive on Mount Desert Island before and after the American Revolution. To earn a living, most settlers fished, built sailing ships, cut down trees to build houses, or farmed.

In the 1850s, rich people began spending their summer

Two views of Acadia and Maine in the 1800s: (above) Artwork from 1850 showing two women walking in Bar Harbor, Maine, while an artists looks on. (right) Cave of the Sea, Schooner Head in the 1870s before large hotels were built on Acadia National Park.

vacations on Mount Desert Island. At first, these summer visitors stayed with local families. But by 1880, more than thirty large hotels had been built on the island. Many of America's richest families built huge summer cottages on the island. They also bought large amounts of land. These families later gave their land to the National Park Service to help create a national monument in 1916, and then, in 1919, Acadia National Park.

Plant and Animal Life

The evergreen trees were once king of the forest at Acadia. But they are slow to grow and quick to burn. A great forest fire in 1947 destroyed most of Acadia's evergreens. Many of the large, white pines survived and still tower over the newer growth

This view of the coastline of Mount Desert Island as seen from Cedar Swamp Mountain shows the 1947 fire did not destroy all of Acadia's evergreens.

forest. The new forest was taken over by birch, maple, and aspen trees. You can still find many evergreens if you visit Acadia, but they are small.

Paper birch trees (left) and making a birch bark canoe (right).

The paper birch is a common tree at Acadia. It has a tough, white bark that was used by the Wabanaki people to make baskets, canoes, and wigwams. The sugar maple

Acadia has many sugar maple trees (left). Blueberries (right) grow throughout Acadia National Park.

can also be found throughout Acadia. Its sweet sap makes that famous New England maple syrup!

Blueberries grow wild all over Acadia. Blueberry picking is permitted in Acadia, but you may pick only enough for yourself!

In autumn, this maple tree creates a striking contrast to the evergreen trees that surround it.

The leaves of these shrubs turn many different colors in the fall. The birch and aspen leaves turn a golden yellow. The maples turn a bright red or orange. Even the blueberry leaves turn a brilliant crimson color.

There is also plenty of plant and marine life at the shoreline. These plants and animals have had to adapt to Acadia's extreme tides. Tides change twice a day and are usually between 10 and 12 feet (3 and

Seaweed and barnacles can be found along Acadia's coast.

3.7 meters) high! Kelp, a dense, brown seaweed, lives just below the low water mark. Crabs, sea urchins, sea anemones, and starfish often live under the kelp plant.

Most animals at Acadia are experts at not being noticed, so you will have to look closely (and quietly) to find them.

The white-tailed deer can be seen in open fields at dawn or dusk, and often during the day. It is tall and graceful with a tan coat and white tail and belly.

White-tailed deer and red fox are among the animals that can be found in Acadia.

The red fox can also be seen at night. The red fox hunts hare and small rodents in open fields and salt marshes. It has pointed ears and a bushy tail.

The playful harbor seal is easily spotted at low tide, lying in the sun on offshore ledges and islands. Harbor seals are 5 to 6 feet (1.5 to 1.8 m) long and have gray-brown fur.

The harbor seal is a favorite animal of park visitors.

The snowshoe hare is probably the animal that is the best prepared for Acadia's harsh winters. When cold weather is near, this mammal sheds its gray-brown coat and grows white fur. This white fur hides the snowshoe hare from predators in the winter snow. The toes of its rear feet spread out to form natural "snowshoes."

Acadia is also home to more than three hundred species of sea, shore, and land birds.

LOBSTERS

The lobster is the most famous of all the many creatures that live in Maine's cold ocean waters. It lives on the ocean floor.

Lobsters are caught in box-shaped wire traps that lie on the ocean floor. Brightly colored buoys mark the ends of ropes attached to the traps. You can see these colorful buoy markers bobbing up and down on the ocean surface all over Acadia's coast.

Lobster meat is found in the powerful front claws, the large tail, and the spindly legs. It tastes sweet and juicy. It is worth all the effort it takes to catch, cook, and eat a lobster!

Your Visit to Acadia

Most of Acadia's scenic view-points can be seen by car on Park Loop Road. Park Loop Road is 20 miles (32 kilometers) long and winds through most of Acadia National Park. But to hear the crashing waves at Thunder Hole and to feel the ocean spray at Otter Cliffs,

Follow Park Loop Road along the water.

Thunder Hole can be very noisy!

you will have to hike a short distance.

Timing is everything at Thunder Hole. The wind pushes the ocean and the tide into this narrow cave.

Pink granite, quartz, and feldspar contribute to the beauty of Otter Cliffs.

The air from the wind becomes trapped, and then escapes with a thunderous roar.

Otter Cliffs are 100-foot (30.5-meter)-tall pink rock formations that rise up straight

Sand Beach attracts many tourists.

from the water. Be careful! The rocks are slippery when wet.

Sand Beach is Acadia's only sandy beach. But don't plan on swimming. The ocean temperature is hardly ever above 55°F (12.7°C). The sand here is mixed with tiny shell pieces, which gives it a crunchy feeling.

Cadillac Mountain is the tallest mountain in Acadia. The top of Cadillac Mountain

Tourists relax on top of Cadillac Mountain.

is 1,530 feet (466 m). It's also the tallest mountain on the North Atlantic coast. You can hike to the top, or drive up on Park Loop Road. On a clear day, you can see the whole park and the mainland of Maine.

Somes Sound is the only fjord on the East Coast of the United States. Steep mountains lie on both sides of the Sound. The Sound is a 168-foot (51-m)-deep gorge of

A lovely view of Somes Harbor at dawn.

salt water that was carved out by glaciers.

Schoodic Point is a colorful rock formation facing the ocean. The high tides pound

away at Schoodic Point. This pounding sends sheets of ocean spray into the air. But pay attention. If you get too close, you will quickly get soaked!

The Carriage Roads

The carriage
roads were
built for
visitors
who do
not want
to drive an
automobile
through the park.
No motor vehicles are
allowed on the carriage roads. They are used
by hikers, horseback riders, horse carriage
riders, and bicycle riders. Handsome bridges
are found throughout the 45-mile (72-km)
stretch of carriage roads.

However you choose to
spend your time at Acadia
National Park, your visit will
be an adventure you will
never forget!

Hiking (opposite page), biking (top), horseback riding (middle), and cross-country skiing (bottom) are just a few of the activities Acadia National Park has to offer.

To Find Out More

Here are some additional resources to help you learn more about Acadia National Park, national parks in general, and Maine.

Books

Fradlin, Dennis B. **Maine.** Children's Press, 1994.

Haaland, Lynn. **Acadia Seacoast:** A Guidebook for Appreciation. Oceanus Institute, Inc., 1988.

Hallet, Bill and Hallet, Jane. **National Park Service: Activities and Adventures for Kids.** Look & See Pubns., 1991.

Marsh, Carole. **Maine Coastales!** Gallopade: Publishing Group, 1996

Marsh, Carole. **Maine "Jography." A Fun Run Through Our State!** Gallopade: Publishing Group, 1994.

Thompson, Kathleen. **Maine.** Raintree Steck-Vaughn Publishers, 1996.

Organizations and Online Sites

Acadia National Park
P.O. Box 177
Bar Harbor, ME 04609
http://www.nps.gov/acad

The National Park Service
U.S. Dept. of the Interior
1849 C Street N.W.
Washington, DC 20240
http://www.nps.gov

General information on all of the national parks.

National Park Foundation
1101 17th Street N.W.,
Suite 1008
Washington, DC 20036

A nonprofit organization that provides private funding for the enhancement and improvement of the national park system. Supports the National Park Service through educational programs and published materials.

Eastern National
446 North Lane
Conshohocken, PA 19428
http://www.easternnational. org/

Provides quality educational products and services to America's national parks.

Friends of Acadia
P.O. Box 725
Bar Harbor, ME 04609

Helps protect Acadia. They have raised more than three million dollars so far to help preserve and protect the beautiful carriage roads.

The National Parks and Conservation Association (NPCA)
1776 Massachusetts Ave. N.W.
Washington, DC 20036

Strives to ensure adequate park funding, the expansion of park boundaries where possible, and the adoption of wiser conservation policies.

Important Words

glaciers huge sheets of ice that move slowly across land or mountains

Jesuit a member of a Roman Catholic religious order

mission headquarters for a group of people sent by a religious group to spread its religion

scavenger an animal that eats waste and decaying things

smallpox a virus that causes high fever and skin bumps

wigwam an American Indian dwelling made of dome-shaped wood poles and bark

Index

(**Boldface** page numbers
   indicate illustrations.)

Bar Harbor, **16**
barnacles, **23**
basalt, 8
beaches, 6. *See also* Sand
   Beach
birch trees. *See* paper
   birch trees
blueberries, 21, **21**
bridges, **41**
Cadillac Mountain, 35, **36,**
   37
carriage roads, **40,** 41
Cave of the Sea, **16**
coastline, 6–8, **7, 9,** 23.
   See also Otter Cliffs;
   Thunder Hole
Eagle Lake, 9
Echo Lake, 9
European settlers, 15
evergreen trees, 18–19,
   19, 22
fjords, 10
glaciers, 9
granite, 8, **9**

harbor seals, 26, **26**
Isle au Haut, 6
Jesuit priests, 12, 14–15, **14**
Jordan Pond, 9
lobsters, 28–29, **29**
Long Pond, 9
map, **4**
marine life, 23–24, 26, 28
Mount Desert Island,
   5–6, 12, **13,** 15, 17
Otter Cliffs,
   10, 30, 32–33, **33,** 35
paper birch trees, 20, **20**
Park Loop Road, 30, **31,** 37
red fox, 25, **25**
Sand Beach, 11, **11, 34,** 35
Schoodic Peninsula, 5
Schoodic Point, 38–39, **39**
snowshoe hare, 27
Somes Harbor, 38
Somes Sound, 10, **10,** 37
sports, **42–43**
sugar maple trees, 20–21,
   21, 22
Thunder Hole, 30, 32–33, **32**
Wabanaki people, 12, 14–15
white-tailed deer, 24, **25**

Meet the Author

Wende Fazio's interest in America's national parks began when she drove cross-country and back again from New Jersey. On that trip, she was enthralled with the awesome beauty and vast wilderness of the many national parks of the east and west. Acadia and Everglades National Parks are particularly special to her. She and her husband, John, spend much of their free time hiking and photographing the national parks and wilderness areas of America.

Wende has written on a variety of subjects. *Acadia National Park* and *Everglades National Park* are her first books with Children's Press.